CUBESATS

and Other Satellite Tech

Co-published by agreement between Shi Tu Hui and World Book, Inc.

Shi Tu Hui
Room 1807, Block 1,
#3 West Dawang Road
Chaoyang District, Beijing 100025
P.R. China

World Book, Inc
180 North LaSalle Street
Suite 900
Chicago, Illinois 60601
USA

Library of Congress Cataloging-in-Publication Data for this volume has been applied for.

Cool Tech (set #2)
ISBN: 978-0-7166-5387-5 (set, hc)

Cubesats and Other Satellite Tech
ISBN: 978-0-7166-5391-2 (hc)

Also available as:
ISBN: 978-0-7166-5397-4 (e-book)
ISBN: 978-0-7166-5403-2 (soft cover)

Written by Richard Spilsbury

STAFF

VP, Editorial: Tom Evans

Manager, New Product: Nicholas Kilzer

Curriculum Designer: Caroline Davidson

Proofreader: Nathalie Strassheim

Coordinator, Design Development & Production:
  Brenda Tropinski

Senior Media Editor: Rosalia Bledsoe

Developed with World Book by
White-Thomson Publishing LTD
www.wtpub.co.uk

ACKNOWLEDGMENTS

Cover © 3Dsculptor/Shutterstock
5 © Artsiom Petrushenka, Alamy Images
6-7 © FoxPictures/Shutterstock; Alexandre Montes, U.S. Air Force
8-9 SpaceX   ; © Virgin Orbit; Cory Huston, NASA; NASA
10-11 © 3Dsculptor/Shutterstock; © Cosmic Shielding Corporation; © FoxPictures/Shutterstock; © TNO; © AAC Clyde Space
12-13 Dominic Hart, NASA; © GomSpace; NASA/JPL-Caltech; © Starfish Space
14-15 © Alejo Miranda, Shutterstock; © Voyager Space; © Guo Zhongzheng, Xinhua/Alamy Images
16-17 © NicoElNino/Shutterstock; © Amazon
18-19 © Terran Orbital Corporation; © GaudiLab/Shutterstock; © Arctic Astronautics; © AST SpaceMobile
20-21 SpaceX; © Swarm Technologies; © Shannon Stapleton, Reuters/Alamy Images
22-23 © The Yomiuri Shimbun, AP Photo; © NaruFoto/Shutterstock
24-25 Aidan Arnold and collaborators, University of Strathclyde; © Skycolors/Shutterstock; © DJI; © Margus Vilbas Photography/Shutterstock

26-27 © aappp/Shutterstock; © Hexagon; Joe Bullinger, U.S. Navy; © cleanfotos/Shutterstock
28-29 © Lockheed Martin; © Alejo Miranda, Shutterstock
30-31 © Eric Lafforgue, Alamy Images; USGS; © SmartSole; © Monkey Business Images/Shutterstock
32-33 USGS; © M-Production/Shutterstock
34-35 © Netfalls Remy Musser, Shutterstock; ESA/Mlabspace (CC BY-SA 3.0 IGO); © Joko P/Shutterstock; © Terry Kelly, Shutterstock; © Pukhov K/Shutterstock
36-37 © Thales Alenia Space; © Polar Geospatial Center; © Stocktrek Images, Inc./Alamy Images; © Warner Bros.; © Mykhailo Pavlenko, Shutterstock
38-39 © Planet Labs Inc.; © Serg64/Shutterstock; CNES; © Senderistas/Shutterstock
40-41 ESA & NASA/Solar Orbiter/EUI & STIX Teams; ESA/Medialab
42-43 © Lockheed Martin; Chris Gunn, NASA; NASA/ESA/CSA/STScI/NIRCam
44-45 © Moviestore Collection Ltd/Alamy Images; NASA/JPL-Caltech; NASA/Johns Hopkins, APL/Steve Gribben

CONTENTS

Acknowledgments....................................2

Glossary 4

Introduction......................................5

(1) CubeSats 6

(2) Telecommunications............................ 16

(3) Navigation.................................... 22

(4) Earth Observation 32

(5) Observing Space 40

Resources 46

Index.. 48

There is a glossary of terms on the first page. Terms defined in the glossary are in boldface type that **looks like this** on their first appearance on any spread (two facing pages).

GLOSSARY

3D printing a variety of manufacturing technologies that create three-dimensional (3D) objects from computer models.

app short for software application that enables a human user to perform some task or activity.

bandwidth the capacity for data transmissions over a network or between devices.

bus outer frame of a satellite.

drone an uncrewed aerial vehicle. Most drones are piloted by remote control.

fiber optics thin flexible fibers of glass or other transparent solids to transmit light signals, chiefly for telecommunications.

geostationary orbiting over a fixed position above the equator and therefore at the same rate as the Earth moves.

greenhouse gas a gas that warms the atmosphere by trapping solar heat reflected from Earth's surface, much like the glass in a greenhouse.

laser a device that produces a narrow and intense beam of light of only one wavelength going in one direction.

latency the overall amount of time it takes for information to be transmitted from the source to the destination in a data network.

LEO short for Low Earth Orbit. An orbital path around Earth with an altitude that lies toward the lower end of the range of possible orbits, typically around 1,200 miles (2,000 kilometers) or less.

machine learning the use of computer systems that are able to learn and adapt to new situations without following prewritten instructions.

magnetorquer a system built from electromagnetic coils that controls attitude (position) and stabilization to prevent a satellite from tumbling in space.

modular constructed in similar sizes or with similar units for flexibility and variety in use.

neural network a computer system modeled on the human brain and nervous system.

payload the scientific or technological instrument carried on board a satellite.

piezoelectric the ability of some materials to convert mechanical energy to electric energy, and vice versa.

ping the time it takes for packets to be sent from the local host to a destination computer and back.

radiation energy that moves through space in a form that can be described as waves or particles. Certain kinds of radiation, known as ionizing radiation, can be harmful.

software a general term for computer programs. A computer program consists primarily of a sequence of instructions telling a computer what to do and how to do it.

solar array solar cells—or photovoltaic cells—that are then grouped together to make solar panels.

solar cell a device converting solar radiation into electricity.

wavelength the distance between two peaks or two crests of a wave of light or other electromagnetic energy. The wavelengths of radio waves are measured in meters and X rays in billionths of an inch.

INTRODUCTION

Could you conduct a science experiment in space from the ground? Do you expect an astonishingly fast internet connection at any point on Earth or clear images of far-distant galaxies? How about an accurate rainfall forecast for the next couple of hours? Would you like an alert when a tree in a protected forest is felled? Remarkably, all of these possibilities are a reality because of satellites.

An artificial satellite is an object that continuously orbits Earth. People use them to communicate or study the Earth and universe, forecast weather, assist navigation, and support military activities. Artificial satellites can be bigger than a house. But most new satellites are somewhat small. These new small satellites range from minisatellites, which are no bigger than 1,100 pounds (500 kilograms), to CubeSats weighing just a few pounds. There are even femtosatellites that weigh less than an ounce (28 grams). These tiny satellites can **ping** data from any point on Earth to another. Today, new technology is giving satellites a remarkable array of amazing capabilities. This book looks at the ways in which satellite technology is shaping the world today and how it might affect it in the future.

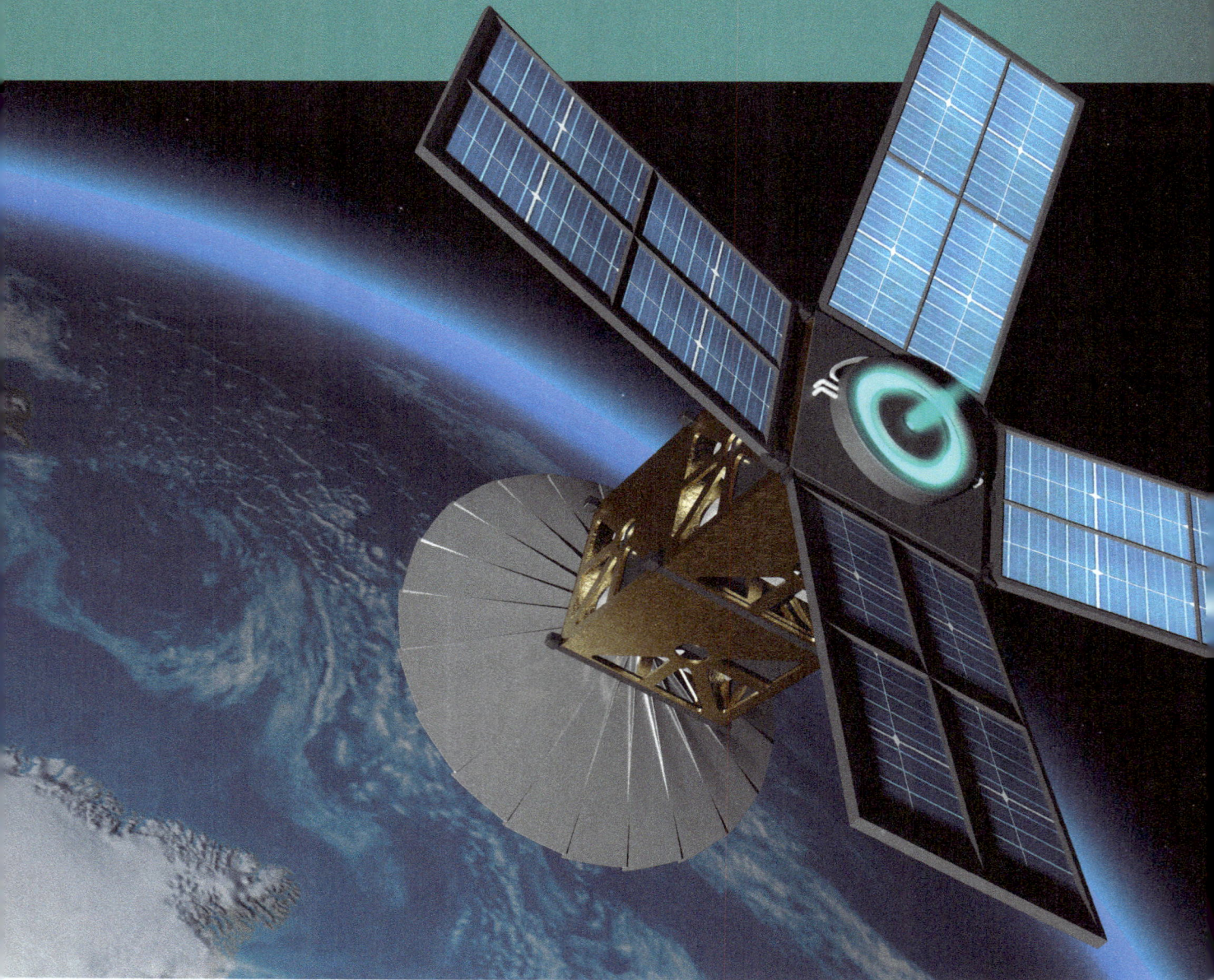

1 CUBESATS

MINI SIZE, MULTIPLE CAPABILITIES

Imagine that you could build your own tiny satellite at home or in a science class. Your design is **modular;** that is, it is constructed of same-sized pieces. Perhaps you could put a science experiment inside to learn about the effects of gravity in orbit. You book a slot on a spaceship online to launch your satellite into space. You then control the satellite's movement and stream data from it using your smartphone.

Remarkably, this capability already exists today in the form of CubeSats. As the name implies, CubeSats are a cube-shaped class of tiny satellites called nanosatellites. They are made up of standard 4-inch (10-centimeter) modular building blocks called units (U). A CubeSat can be as small as a single unit (1U). Designers may add additional cubes depending on the **payload** and function of the satellite. Smaller is always better, because launching satellites into orbit is very expensive. The largest CubeSats are up to 27U. CubeSats are cheaper to build than traditional satellites. They use commercial off-the-shelf (COTS) parts, rather than custom-designed parts. COTS parts can be manufactured in bulk.

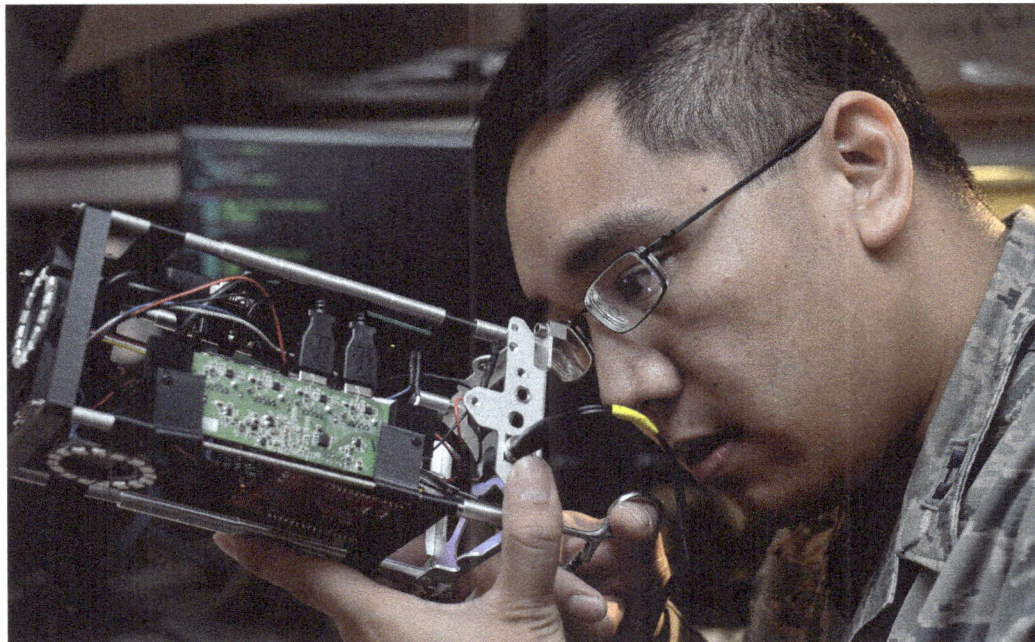

LAUNCHING CUBESATS

A CubeSat may be small and cheap, but to work it must be launched into orbit. That is expensive. Satellites are transported inside a launch vehicle and released when they reach sufficient altitude for the satellite to enter its orbit. Most satellites operate in **LEO** (Low Earth Orbit) between 124 and 1,240 miles (200 and 2,000 kilometers) above Earth. This has traditionally been done via a ground launch using large rockets. Today's smaller satellites may be launched in a new way called air launch.

Air launch. One way to launch a satellite is to attach the launch vehicle to an airplane that carries it to the outer edges of Earth's atmosphere. Virgin Orbit's LauncherOne is a small rocket that can maneuver a satellite to the correct orbit height. It is mounted to the underside of a Boeing 747 and launched from around 35,000 feet (10,600 meters). A company named B2Space has developed an air launch using a rockoon system. Here, a helium balloon lifts a rocket with the satellite payload. The rocket fires the satellite into orbit from a great height. Air launch systems have the advantage that the launch vehicles can operate from any suitable airport runway.

Ground launch on large rockets is the most common way to launch satellites into space. After blastoff, the main stage rocket and boosters drop off once they have used up their fuel. Only the second stage continues to orbit height. After releasing its satellite payload, the second-stage rocket falls away. However, such new reusable rockets as SpaceX Starship work differently. The first stage of this rocket, Super Heavy, has 33 powerful Raptor engines to lift the Starship into orbit. Super Heavy then returns to Earth and lands at the launch site for reuse. The Starship section has an enormous hold that can accommodate up to 100 tons (91 metric tons) of payload. Once it releases a satellite, Starship also returns to Earth for reuse. SpaceX plans to use the Starship to return people to the moon and one day send humans to Mars.

A range of different CubeSats with different payloads secured inside a circular mount. This will be attached to a launch vehicle for transportation to space by rideshare.

Hitching a ride. Deploying a satellite using a dedicated launch allows users to choose the specific launch time and orbit. But it can be very expensive. A cheaper alternative is rideshare. Customers coordinate the construction of their satellites to deploy on the same launch vehicle. The standardized modular units of CubeSats make it possible to pack several together in a single launch vehicle. Other small satellites with varied shapes and payloads can be added on circular motorized mounts that release them into space. Using CubeSats and rideshare launches, companies that once had to pay hundreds of thousands of dollars to put a satellite into orbit can now do the same for a fraction of that price.

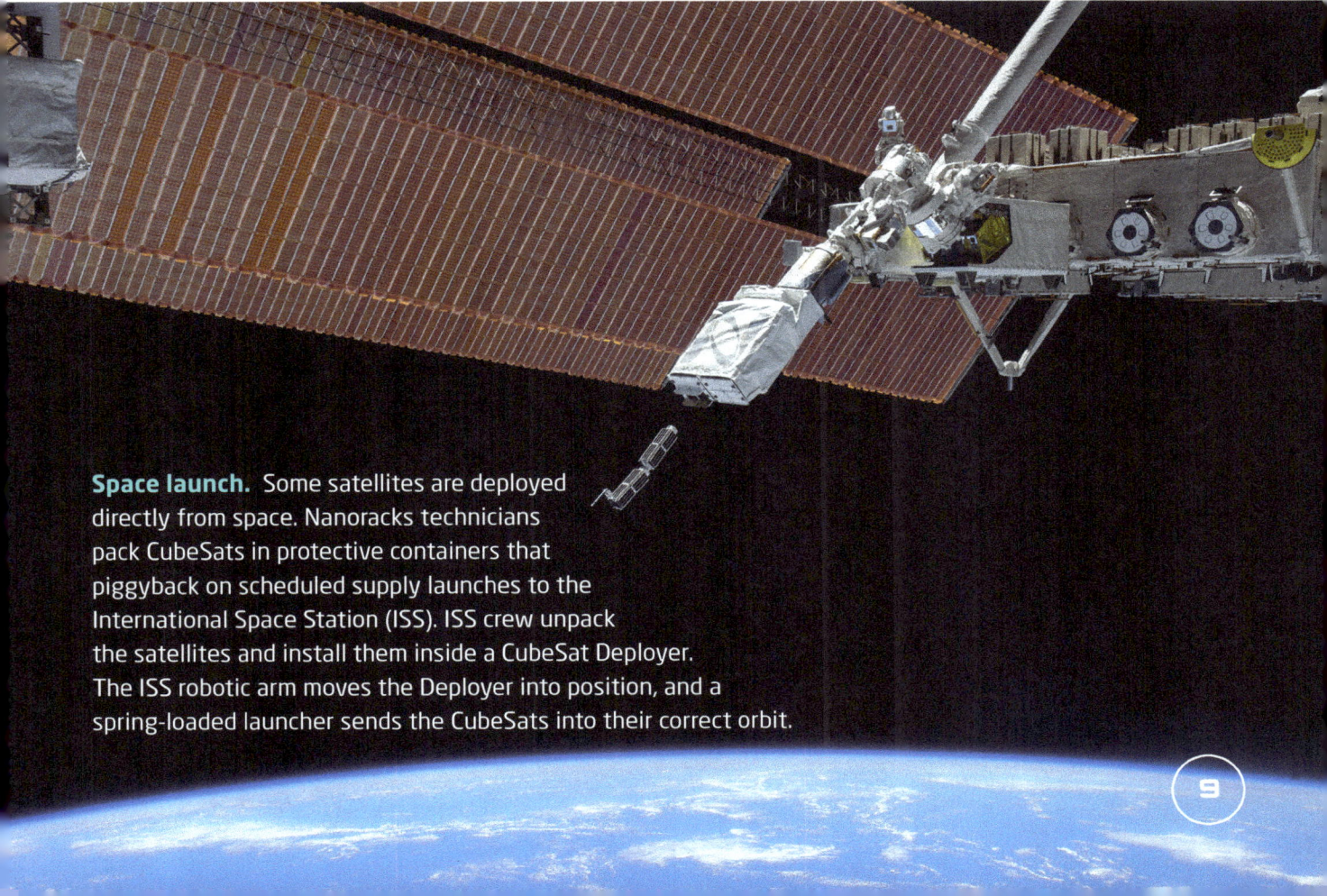

Space launch. Some satellites are deployed directly from space. Nanoracks technicians pack CubeSats in protective containers that piggyback on scheduled supply launches to the International Space Station (ISS). ISS crew unpack the satellites and install them inside a CubeSat Deployer. The ISS robotic arm moves the Deployer into position, and a spring-loaded launcher sends the CubeSats into their correct orbit.

CUBESATS IN OPERATION

The key components of a CubeSat for propulsion, communications, computer system, and the payload must be packed into a protective **bus** (outer frame). The bus must also have a protective shield. Metal shields are strong but can add weight to a CubeSat. Today, lighter composite materials are used to shield delicate components.

Composite shielding. Plasteel is tough enough to withstand impacts by space debris. In LEO, a CubeSat typically travels at around 17,000 miles per hour (10,560 kilometers per hour). At that speed, hitting any debris in the same orbit could cause catastrophic damage. Plasteel also shields the CubeSat interior from damaging **radiation** that can ruin materials inside a satellite. Plasteel is easy to manufacture into satellite-specific shapes using **3D printing.**

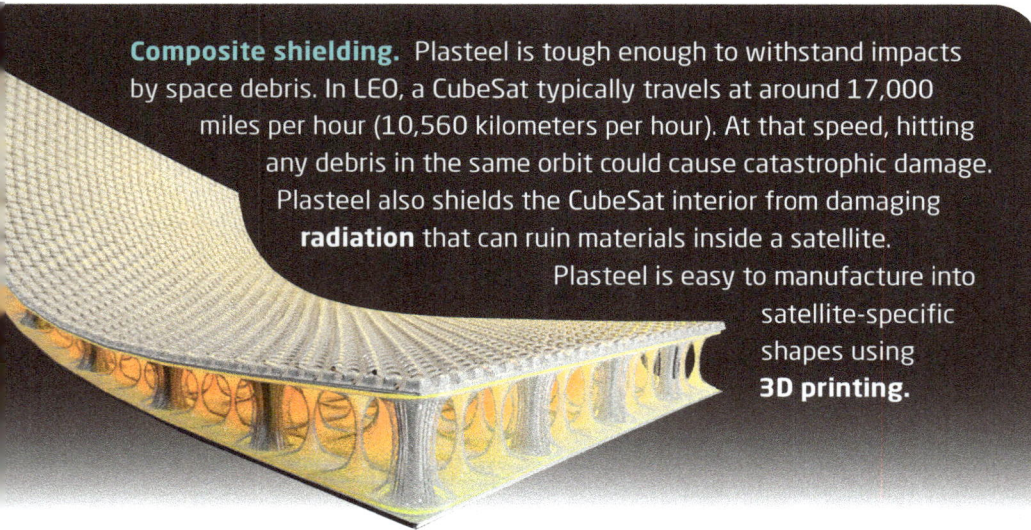

Solar power. Like most spacecraft, CubeSats rely on **solar cells** to generate power. Some CubeSat exteriors are coated in solar cells. Others use larger **solar arrays** resembling wings. PHOTON CubeSat arrays from AAC Clyde Space use efficient XTJ Prime solar cells on a lightweight aluminum support structure. These cells operate at cooler temperatures and use a wider range of the solar spectrum than other commonly available cells. They generate power for more of each day. Built-in sensors orient the CubeSat, so that the arrays always face the sun.

Solar arrays fold flat during transportation into space, where they deploy to full extension.

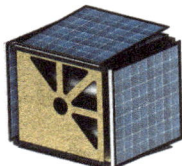

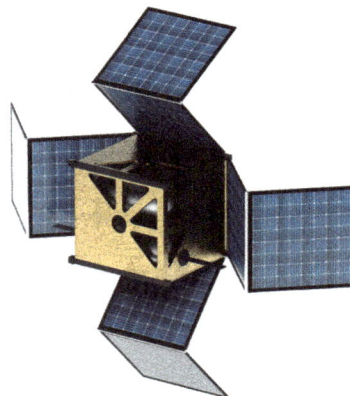

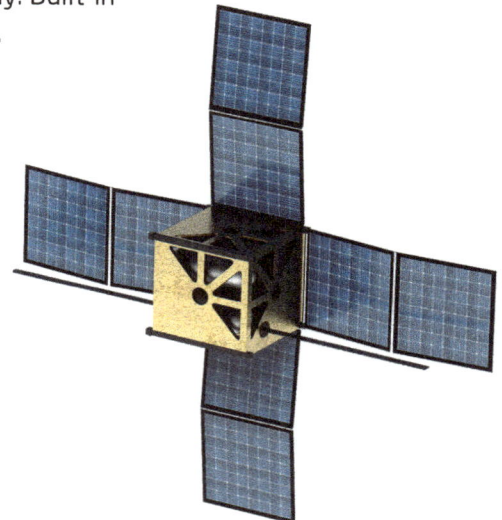

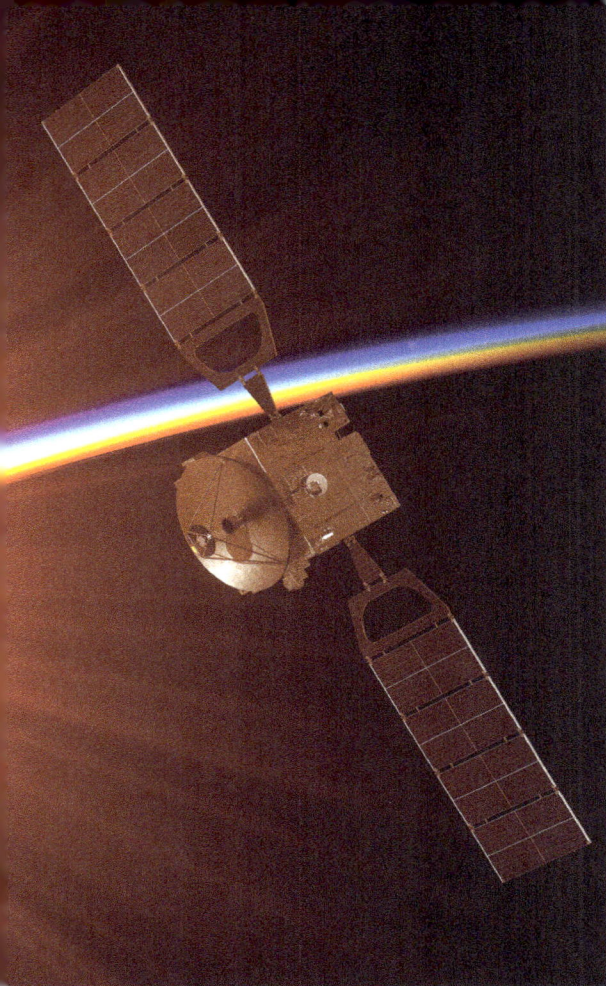

The right attitude. An attitude determination and control system (ADCS) is required to point a CubeSat in a chosen direction, such as to orient solar cells toward the sun. The ADCS contains attitude sensors that calculate where the satellite is currently pointing and attitude actuators that rotate the satellite in the desired direction. The AAC Clyde Space IADCS400 contains an integrated star tracker that recognizes certain stars to calculate its position. Three **magnetorquers** control pitch, roll, and yaw. A modern ADCS takes up almost 1U, so most CubeSats comprise several units.

Smart CubeSat. The Piezoelectric Assisted Smart Structure (PEASS) CubeSat contains **fiber optic** sensors that measure changes in materials and sensitive electronics. In orbit, a CubeSat is exposed to incredible temperature changes, from 212 °F to -58 °F (100 °C to -50 °C). This can deform the outer skin and interior components. Over time, this movement can damage parts and cause system malfunction. Smart **software** in the PEASS CubeSat analyzes temperature changes and instructs **piezoelectric** actuators to adjust deformed parts into the correct alignment. The piezoelectric system generates power for the actuators using mechanical stress and heat.

CUBESATS AT WORK

CubeSats can be deployed as standalone satellites or as part of a coordinated group that works together called a swarm. Swarm CubeSats have onboard technology to determine their proximity to each other to avoid collisions. The United States National Aeronautics and Space Administration (NASA) CubeSat Proximity Operations and Demonstration (CPOD) mission in 2022 sent two 3U CubeSats into orbit. The CubeSats could move autonomously toward each other and coordinated movements to dock together.

Close proximity coordination. Key to satellite swarm coordination is a module with four sensors to detect visible and infrared (IR) radiation in narrow and wide fields of view. The sensors record images of the nearby satellite. Onboard computer vision algorithms compare the images to digital catalogs of satellite shapes. The computer determines the trajectory the satellite takes to move close to another satellite in the swarm. The CPOD mission demonstrated only two CubeSats orbiting together, but the same technology can be used in large swarms of CubeSats.

Mini labs are ideal payloads for scientific research using CubeSats. For example, NASA's 2022 BioSentinel mission sent a 6U CubeSat containing mini labs beyond Earth's orbit more than 650,000 miles (1.5 million kilometers) into space. The CubeSat held dried yeast samples that were exposed to the radiation of deep space. Scientists are studying how yeast cells respond to radiation. The data will help them understand how people might survive on long missions in deep space. Special dyes measure the yeast cell activity in the mini lab. BioSentinel detects any changes and transmits the data to Earth.

Support sats. CubeSats can be deployed to support the operations of spacecraft, too. A mission in 2018 sent a lander named *InSight* to the surface of Mars. Two CubeSats—MarCO-A and MarCO-B—were used as communications relays on the mission. Their sensors detected *InSight's* movement through the Martian atmosphere and at landing. They provided a real-time communications link to Earth when *InSight* could not send data itself.

Orbit repair shops. In a satellite swarm, older CubeSats may need to be removed and replaced. Otherwise, they may become part of the growing mass of space junk. Starfish Space's Otter Pup, due for operation in 2023, is a prototype repair satellite that will correct a satellite that has gone off course. It carries a sticky apparatus that can attach itself to a target satellite. Otter Pup can then push the satellite back into the correct orbit. If the satellite needs to be removed, Otter Pup will push it out of orbit to burn up in Earth's atmosphere.

13

SPACE STATIONS

Look skyward on a clear night, and you may see one of the biggest satellites ever made. The Chinese Space Station (CSS) will orbit Earth from 211 to 280 miles (340 to 450 kilometers) for decades. CSS is the most modern space station around and the crowning achievement of China's space program. Like other orbiting stations, CSS was built in space by connecting several smaller modules.

Core module. The core module of the CSS is the *Tianhe*. The name means "harmony of the heavens" in Chinese. This is the CSS management and control center. It measures 54 feet (17 meters) long and weighs 24 tons (22 metric tons). It was launched into LEO in 2021 on a Chinese Long March V rocket. *Tianhe* has facilities to house three taikonauts (space travelers). The CSS interior is uncluttered, with wireless devices replacing devices requiring cables. It has advanced life-support systems. These include a water supply system that can extract drinking water from urine. Five ports on *Tianhe* can be used to dock visiting spacecraft or add other modules.

Tianhe core module

Research module

Research modules. Space stations are important places for scientific research. Two CSS modules designed for research, named *Wentian* and *Mengtian,* were launched in 2022. The modules maneuvered near *Tianhe,* where its robotic arm moved them to its docking ports, creating a T-shaped structure. Spacewalking taikonauts connected the modules.

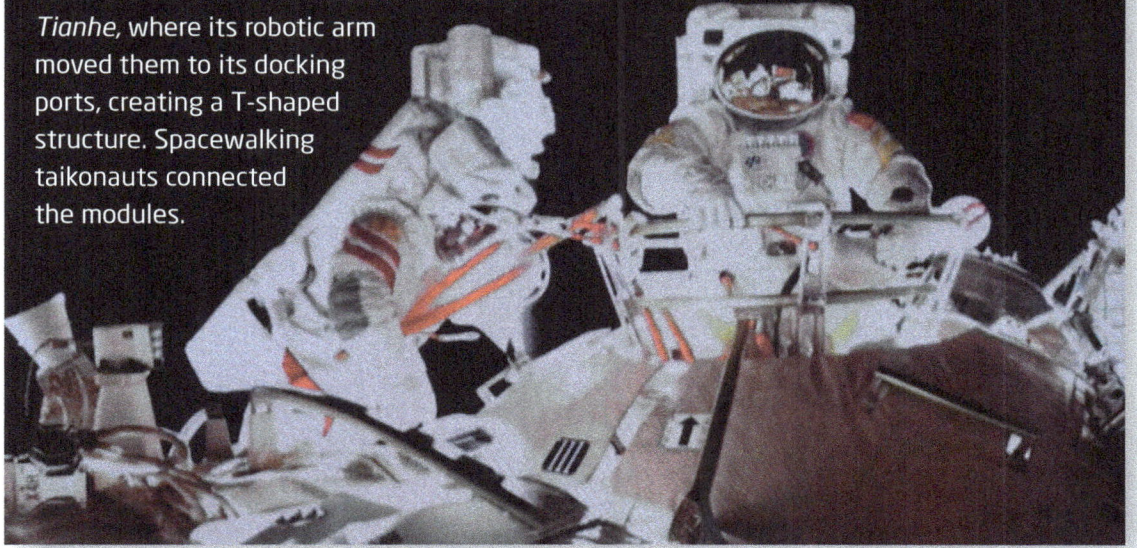

Racks inside each CSS module house a variety of scientific experiments. Each module has a power supply, computer network, and cooling systems needed for experiments. Outside the modules, there are docking points for CubeSats to connect. Hundreds of experiments are planned. One will study phase changes between gases and liquids in low gravity (microgravity). This experiment will help develop small, efficient cooling systems for spacecraft and other uses here on Earth.

Future stations. ISS was the main space science station for decades, hosting hundreds of astronauts and thousands of experiments. But ISS will reach the end of its operational life by 2030. By 2028, Voyager Space intends to launch a commercial space station named Starlab into LEO. Starlab's orbiting laboratory will have research links with scientists in the United States. By then, NASA's Gateway, a modular space station orbiting the Moon, will be underway. NASA plans to use Gateway as a moon base for research and future space exploration.

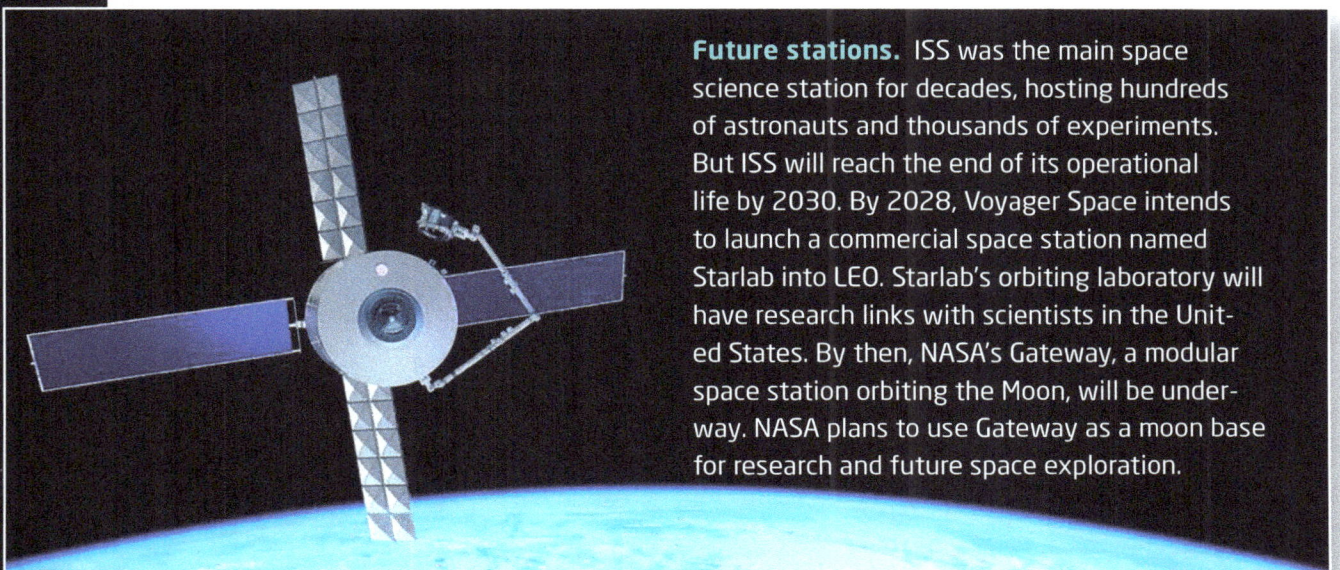

2 TELECOMMUNICATIONS

TOMORROW'S TELECOMS

We are now almost 70 years into the era of satellite tele-communication. The pace of change has been incredible. Large dish antennae receiving weak signals relayed from massive satellites could transmit only telephone calls and black-and-white television signals. These have been replaced with new compact receivers providing vastly more complex information. Today's satellite telecommunications systems transmit everything from telemedicine consultations to instant live feeds of breaking global news.

Amazon's Kuiper satellite receiver dish is about 12 inches (30 centimeters) in diameter. Unlike a traditional satellite dish, Kuiper can transmit and receive signals. Kuiper uses overlapping banks of antennae known as phased array for both functions. The dish transmits and receives signals at different **wavelengths.** In the Kuiper dish, signals from the multiple antennae move through a single aperture (outlet) to create a focused beam of radio waves. This tiny device can stream video in an instant. The phased array reduces size, weight, and manufacturing costs compared to larger traditional satellite dishes.

TELECOM SATELLITES IN OPERATION

Radio waves transmitting data travel hundreds to thousands of miles between telesatellites and Earth. Radio waves transmitted over a greater distance have a greater **latency,** or lag, that delays the receipt of information. A cable internet signal may have a latency of 30 milliseconds (ms), while the same signal from a satellite might be 600 ms. That doesn't seem like much. But today's internet and other advanced technologies demand near-instant communication of huge amounts of data. Scientists are developing new satellite technology to satisfy that demand.

Laser communications. In 2022, NASA's TBIRD (Terabyte Infrared Delivery) system, a 3U CubeSat, sent data by **laser** at 200 gigabits per second (Gbps) from LEO to a ground station on Earth. This was the fastest transmission rate ever demonstrated by an optical (light-using) communications satellite. Laser communications use infrared light to pack and send more information per transmission than radio waves. About the size of a shoebox, TBIRD can transmit more data faster than a traditional satellite many times its size. Future satellites and spacecraft will benefit from this technology to transfer and downlink data at incredible speeds.

Bandwidth breakthrough. ViaSat satellites will soon be offering fast in-flight Wi-Fi (wireless internet) via the Ka band. Some of the newest telecommunication technology uses the high-frequency Ka band because it has a wide **bandwidth** between 27 and 40 GHz (gigahertz). Here, there is less signal congestion, which allows higher and faster data transmission rates than other bands. ViaSat can deliver data to airplanes in-flight more effectively. Small aircraft antennae can receive high-speed data because the Ka wavelengths are so small. The first operational model, ViaSat-3A, was deployed in 2022. It streams data to flights over the Americas. Future ViaSat networks will provide high-speed internet communications for all global flight paths.

Orbiting cell towers are a new concept in communications satellites. BlueWalker 3 from AST provides direct-to-cell phone connectivity without ground-based antennae. This satellite is about one-third the size of a tennis court. Much of the bulk is two large solar arrays and several antennae to send signals. BlueWalker 3 provides quality coverage in remote or undeveloped locations where there are fewer cell towers or where signals are blocked by hills. One drawback of this technology is that BlueWalker 3 transmits powerful radio waves at frequencies used for cell phones. These waves may interfere with radio telescopes and other radio technology on Earth.

WoodSat. First launched in 2021, WoodSat is an inexpensive CubeSat alternative to BlueWalker 3. Amazingly, WoodSat has a tough bus made of plywood! WoodSat's payload includes an amateur radio relay system. Users can purchase an inexpensive ground station **app** on their smartphone to uplink and downlink low-bandwidth radio signals and images globally.

COMMUNICATIONS CONSTELLATIONS

Some of today's most cutting-edge communications satellites orbit in large groups or constellations. Hundreds of identical satellites provide wider signal coverage to deliver high-speed streaming, video gaming, and video calls virtually anywhere on Earth.

Starlink is SpaceX's constellation of sleek telecom satellites. Orbiting in LEO, data can ping from ground to satellite and back in 20 milliseconds. A typical **geostationary** satellite at 22,000 miles (35,400 kilometers) would take around 12 times as long. The high-speed data transfer and lower latency provide fast broadband internet. The Starlink constellation is growing fast using SpaceX launch vehicles to reach orbit. They serve a growing customer base, especially in remote areas not served by Earth-based broadband internet. SpaceX also operates a private constellation named Starshield. Satellites in Starshield can encrypt sensitive information, so that government agencies can communicate over a secure network.

Collision avoidance. Starlink satellites have krypton ion thrusters that can adjust their orbit and also avoid collision with other satellites in the constellation. These lightweight electronic thrusters are controlled by an autonomous (self-controlled) collision avoidance system. The system begins evasive maneuvers if sensors identify even the slightest chance of collision. Starlink satellites are designed for disposal, too. They are constructed to fall and burn up in Earth's atmosphere at the end of their service life. This way, they do not create dangerous space junk.

Race for satellite internet. There is a lot of money to be made in the competitive satellite broadband market. SpaceX already has a constellation of more than 3,200 satellites and plans to launch nearly 30,000. But Amazon and other competitors are planning similar constellations. Amazon's first Kuiper satellites will launch in 2023 on a Vulcan Centaur rocket. Amazon plans to complete its constellation by building up to 4 satellites per day, which will be sent into orbit on nearly 50 rocket launches.

SpaceBEEs. SpaceX has expanded its range of constellations with its Swarm Technologies SpaceBEEs (Basic Electronic Elements). These sandwich-sized picosatellites are the smallest CubeSats in space, measuring just 0.25U. They make up a growing constellation named Swarm, which sends data to cracker-sized chips called tiles. The tiles are small enough to put inside a wide variety of electronic devices. Swarm is an inexpensive service that provides global satellite connectivity in our increasingly connected world.

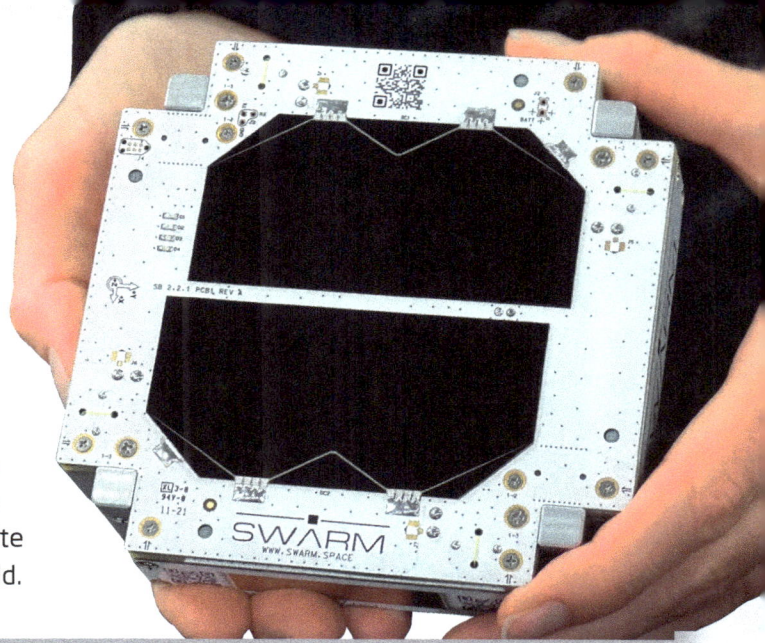

Satellites in conflict. Critical infrastructure in Ukraine, including cable internet and cell services, was damaged in the Russia–Ukraine war that began in 2022. SpaceX supplied Starlink equipment to keep Ukraine connected. This helped Ukraine communicate with the outside world and coordinate its defense. But when Ukraine used Starlink to launch **drone** missile attacks, SpaceX disabled their Starlink. SpaceX claimed Ukraine was weaponizing a communications system and risked escalating the conflict. Some people believe that this decision hindered Ukraine's ability to defend itself.

3 NAVIGATION

FUTURE DIRECTIONS

Navigation is practically unthinkable today without the use of Global Navigation Satellite Systems (GNSS). These are made up of satellite constellations in medium Earth orbits (MEO) 12,550 miles (20,000 kilometers) above a network of ground stations. Today, there are four GNSS on Earth. The most familiar is the United States' Global Positioning System (GPS). But the newest and most accurate GNSS is China's BeiDou constellation.

BeiDou has a constellation of 45 satellites, more than any other GNSS, providing detailed coverage of Earth. At any location, a user has access to 16 satellites that provide real-time location data to a superior resolution of around 3 feet (1 meter). Unlike GPS, which only broadcasts signals to users, BeiDou satellites can receive data from a transmission chip inside cell devices. This capability makes them a preferred GNSS for rescue organizations since they can find people more easily. However, some security experts worry that this same technology may monitor and track the location of individual users of BeiDou's services.

SATELLITE TIMING

Navigation using any GNSS only works because it is a precision timing system. A receiver's position is determined by the transit time of signals traveling at light speed from multiple satellites to the receiver. GNSS satellites have ultraprecise atomic clocks. These clocks measure time based on the vibration of cesium atoms when microwaves are fired at them. They are synchronized to Universal Coordinated Time (UTC), a global time standard derived from precise atomic clocks in laboratories. However, typical satellite clocks can vary by a nanosecond or more. This can cause problems as satellites get out of sync. Location and navigation become less accurate. To remedy this, scientists are developing new atomic clocks for GNSS satellites.

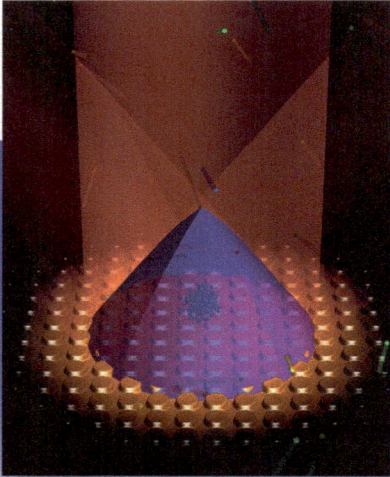

New vibrations. Miniature cold atomic clocks from Wideblue fire laser beams at strontium atoms. Special magneto-optical traps split and steer the light beam into atoms and carefully measure energy levels within them. Regular patterns in the energy levels are translated into time signals. The vibrations in these atoms are up to 100,000 times faster than those of a cesium atomic clock. This faster ticking makes for more accurate timekeeping. A cold atomic clock will not lose one second in 30 million years!

Optimizing aviation. Position, navigation, and timing (PNT) data are critical in the aviation industry. Accurate PNT helps maintain flight schedules, avoid air traffic congestion, and plan optimal routes to reduce fuel consumption. The IRIS program uses 4D technology (latitude, longitude, altitude, and time) using data from Inmarsat GNSS satellites to pinpoint aircraft and their predicted flight path. It transmits this precise real-time positional data to air traffic control, where computers compare it to the original flight plan. Deviations are recognized quickly, and adjustments are made. Such rapid responses help reduce the environmental impact of aviation. For example, using IRIS to take the shortest route at optimal altitude, an aircraft fleet could use about 5 percent less fuel. With thousands of flights every day, that can really add up!

Energy infrastructure. The energy industry relies on PNT capability from GNSS satellites for the timing and synchronization of power generation and distribution within the grid. Many parts of the energy industry infrastructure, from wind turbines to oil and gas pipelines or rigs, exist in remote locations. Today, sensors on turbine blades or pipeline joints can detect signs of damage. The Wyld satellite interface uses low-power sensor-to-satellite technology to uplink data. Software in a Wyld gateway device can downlink the data from satellites in an instant for power companies to assess repairs. The traditional method of uplinking data via wireless networks was often unavailable in remote locations.

Satellite farming uses GNSS to help control farm robots including tractors and drones to aid agricultural efficiency. DJI Agras from DroneAG can spray fertilizer or sow seeds with incredible precision over fields, day or night. It follows a predetermined smart flight path based on digital mapping that ensures it does not sow or spray on the same patch of land, avoiding waste. Databases derived from GPS, soil sampling, and weather data identify particular areas on farms that need more or fewer resources. Computers determine the optimal time to water or fertilize crops to maximize harvest.

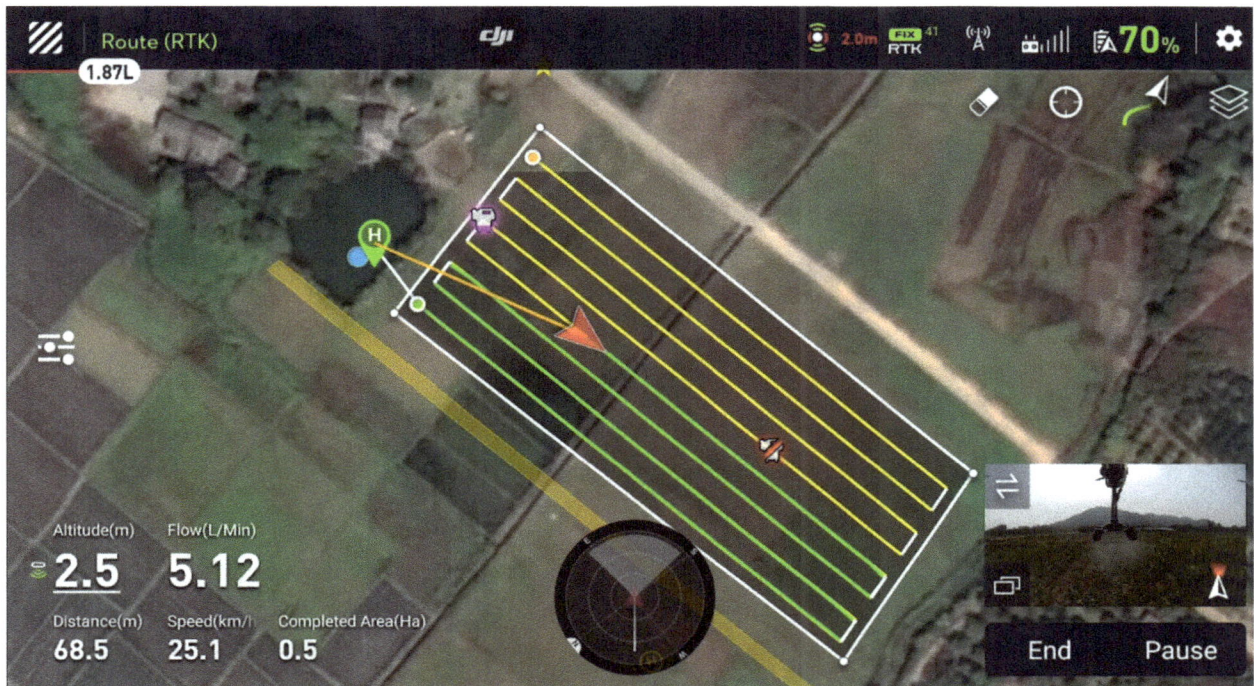

GPS SECURITY

Without GNSS, financial institutions would not be able to time-stamp global trades to a fraction of a second accuracy. This could affect stock market performance and potentially harm financial security. Satellite-tracked missile systems might hit the wrong target. Emergency services might go to the wrong place to help people injured in an accident. A serious problem with GNSS is that the signals used by GNSS satellites are very weak. They are prone to interference from other, more powerful signals. They can also be blocked using inexpensive jamming technology. That is why antijamming technology is vital in the battle to keep PNT operating for everyone.

Jam-canceling antennae. A small electronic signal jammer using just 10 watts can disrupt some GPS receivers up to 20 miles (30 kilometers) away. The solution is to reduce the jamming signal by causing electromagnetic wave interference in the antenna. NovAtel's rugged GPS Anti-Jam Technology (GAJT) antenna provides an uninterrupted signal connection with GPS satellites for military use. The technology allows precise positioning to be maintained for tanks, drones, communications, and other devices on the battlefield. GAJT detects the direction of a jamming signal.

Software for security. In 2022, several Russian cities faced widespread GPS disruption likely caused by *spoofing*. This is when someone creates false GNSS signals to "spoof" a receiver into thinking it is elsewhere. The disruption was probably due to Russian spoofing of GPS coverage, so that Ukrainian armored drones could not locate their targets in Russia. BroadShield is jamming and spoofing detection software from Orolia Defense & Security as part of its Interference, Detection, and Mitigation (IDM) product line.

The software detects interference and small anomalies within a GPS signal. These are telltale signs of spoofing. BroadShield provides an immediate alert, allowing the host system to recalibrate against the jamming or spoofing and nullify the rogue signal.

Encryption is the best way to defend against spoof signals. Encrypting (converting into code) signals almost guarantees that a false duplicate signal cannot be sent to deceive a recipient. M-Code (Military Code) signal technology developed by the United States military has been developed to support encryption and defend against jamming. It also provides better GPS coverage in densely wooded or hilly places. The high-power M-Code signal improves the availability and accuracy of the signal for users. It is a dedicated and more robust GPS signal for military users that is more resilient against interruption from jamming devices.

GPS without satellites. Researchers have developed a new and improved navigation technology that could kick into action should GPS navigation be interrupted—without using satellites! SuperGPS is a navigation system accurate to within 4 inches (10 centimeters). It uses networks similar to cell networks, using fiber-optic and wireless connections. Instead of streaming data to our phones, the network can communicate with and precisely locate devices with highly accurate UTC synchronization with a connected terrestrial laser clock.

GPS IIIF

GPS is one of the older GNSS systems—some of its NAVSTAR satellites were launched 30 years ago! Today, BeiDou matches or exceeds NAVSTAR in accuracy and other capabilities. GNSS is extremely useful for domestic navigation, but it is vital for the modern military. These navigation satellites are three times more accurate than their predecessors. There are six GPS III satellites in operation in MEO today and four more awaiting launch. In 2027, the first of 22 GPS IIIF satellites are planned for launch. These advanced systems will be a major upgrade over the earlier generation.

Longer operation. GPS IIIF satellites are designed to operate for 15 years—about twice as long as current GPS satellites. Their GPS payload is built into Lockheed Martin's LM 2100 Combat Bus, a resilient satellite vehicle originally designed for military use. The bus includes durable mechanical systems to move the solar arrays. They also have improved software, power, and propulsion units. Two LM 2100 units can be launched at one time, which reduces the cost per launch. This bus also has a system port, so GPS IIIF satellites can be upgraded in orbit. This port works a bit like a USB socket. Visiting minisatellites can simply plug in and add new payloads.

3D-printed antennae built into GPS IIIF satellites allow rapid communication with ground stations on Earth. These teardrop-shaped antennae have a unique form produced as a single solid piece. 3D printing a single piece is easier and cheaper compared to older manufacturing methods that involved soldering many separate pieces together. 3D printing also reduces variabilities in the build, effectively removing defects. This makes the antenna more resilient and better able to withstand violent shaking during launch and extreme temperature changes that occur in orbit.

Antijam beam. GPS III and IIIF satellites use spoof and jam-resistant M-code (military code) signals. These signals can be focused in a tight beam aimed at specific areas. Regional Military Protection (RMP) is a concentrated M-code signal that gives up to 60 times greater antijamming capability. This capability is vital if military units are deployed on battlefields where signals are likely to be jammed.

Hostility sensors. Military experts think that space will be the new battlefield. Vital GNSS satellites need to detect and defend from attack. In 2021, Russia tested its antisatellite capabilities by firing a rocket at an old satellite. The explosion created a cloud of space debris, forcing astronauts on the ISS to take shelter from possible debris impact. GPS IIIF satellites have built-in sensors to detect hostile activity. Onboard sensors monitor Earth's atmosphere to detect explosions—even nuclear explosions—from space. Energetic charged particle (ECP) sensors can differentiate ECP's produced naturally and those created by weapons.

TRACKING

PNT data provided by GNSS is also vital for tracking the movements of objects. For example, police can monitor the movement of vehicles in traffic, or customers can find their ride-share driver. Such tracking is also useful in monitoring the natural world. Scientists attach tiny GPS devices to wildlife in collars, backpacks, or implants. GPS tracking helps scientists learn about animal behavior. It can show patterns of movement or migration. A sudden drop in activity may signal that an animal is hibernating.

Smart GPS. There are times when wildlife does not need to be tracked—such as when an animal is sleeping. Smart GPS from Telemetry Solutions uses a built-in accelerometer to distinguish incidental movements during downtime from purposeful movements that need to be tracked. The device saves battery life by not downlinking PNT data from satellites during animal downtime. The device stores PNT data that can be downloaded wirelessly from up to 20 miles (30 kilometers) away.

Earth movements. GPS helps scientists track Earth's movements. For example, vertical and horizontal changes in the ground may indicate a buildup of magma beneath. This may indicate an impending volcanic eruption or earthquake. GPS data can often provide more accurate earthquake predictions than traditional seismographs. In 2011, GPS detected ground movement of 15 feet (5 meters) days before a devastating earthquake and tsunami in Japan. Scientists viewed the inconclusive seismograph data in that same period as a false alarm.

Crowdsourced tracking. Today, scientists can use smartphone data to predict earthquakes more accurately. The MyShake app extracts data from accelerometers in connected phones. These continuously monitor slight movements, day or night. The app uses a **neural network** to distinguish random movements from the vibrations of an earthquake. If the vibrations fit the profile of an earthquake, the app relays the information—with GPS coordinates—to the Berkeley Seismological Laboratory in California. The lab sends out earthquake alerts if necessary. This crowdsourced system can detect earthquakes down to magnitude 5 within around 6 miles (10 kilometers) of the epicenter.

Vulnerable people can also benefit from new GPS applications. Receivers built into smartwatches or tags carried by children can help parents locate them. SmartSole is a GPS-tracking device hidden inside shoes. It is designed to help prevent people with dementia from wandering into dangerous situations. Caregivers can use a SmartSole app to set a geozone (perimeter) around a residence where wearers can safely move. If a wearer leaves the geozone, an alert is sent to the caregiver's smartphone, so they can lead them to safety.

4 EARTH OBSERVATION

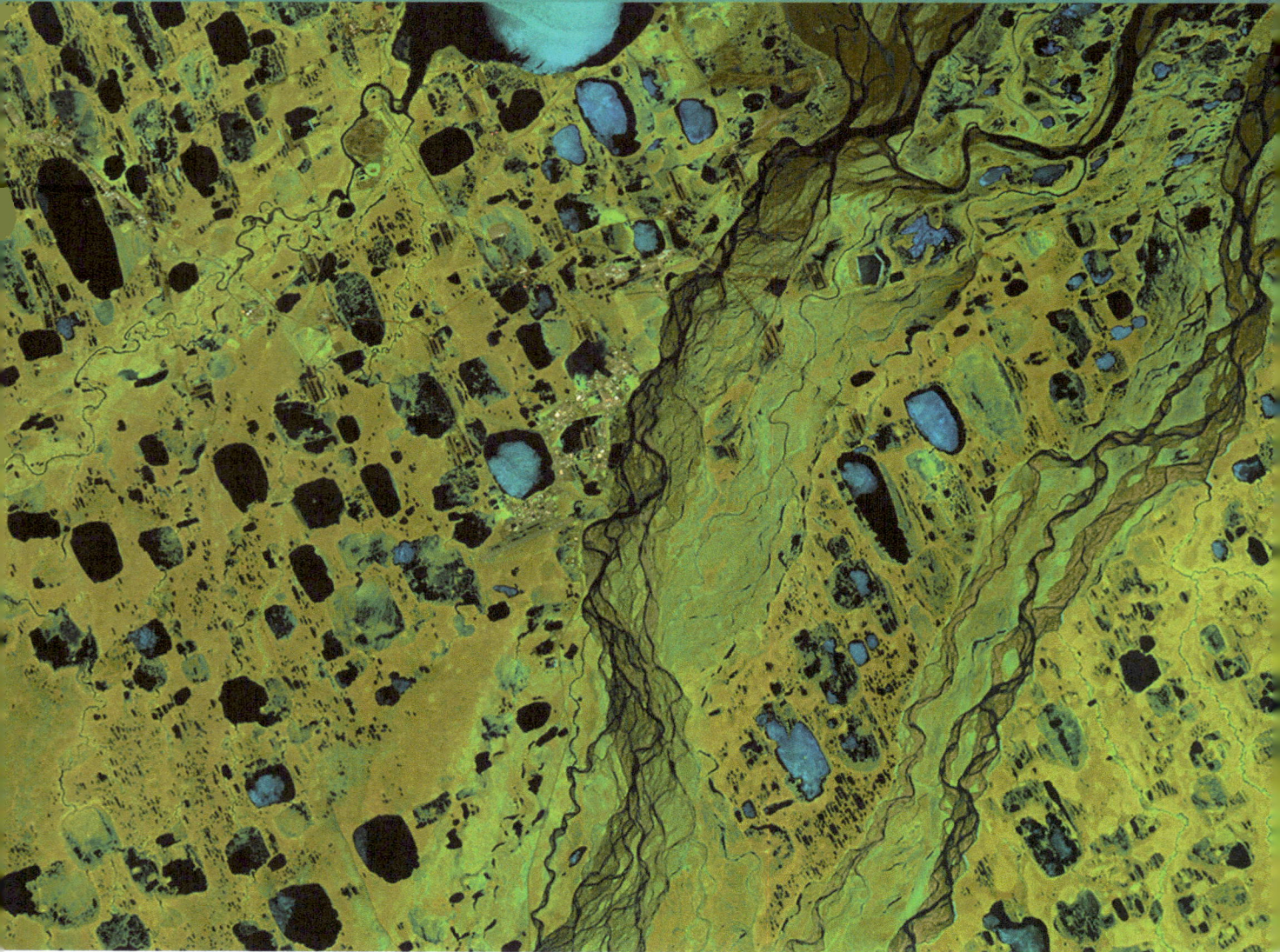

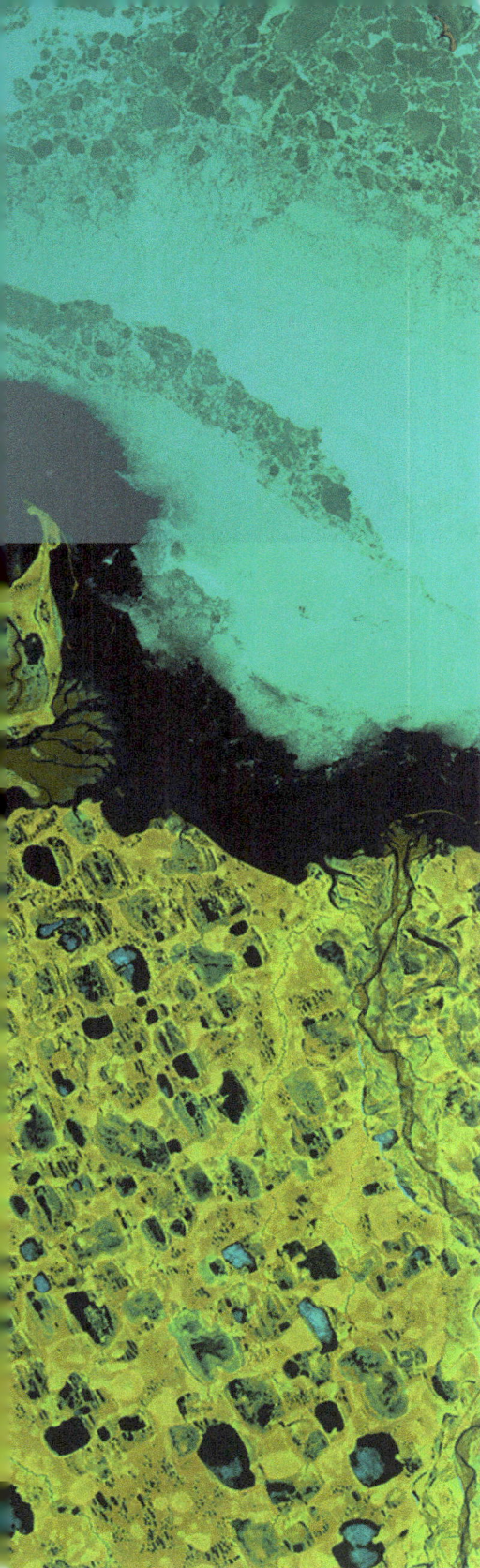

PLANET WATCH

New satellites play an important role in monitoring and learning about Earth's weather patterns and extreme events, land cover, and resources. Data from new Earth-observing satellites inform us about climate change and help guide disaster response. Today's modern satellites examine Earth in detail via remote sensing (monitoring the physical characteristics of an area using its reflected and emitted radiation at a distance). Landsat satellites are some of the most advanced remote sensing satellites around.

The Landsat 9 satellite began operation in 2021, orbiting 438 miles (705 kilometers) above Earth. Its payload collects around 1,400 new images every day. Its state-of-the-art Operational Land Imager (OLI) senses visible light and near-shortwave infrared wavelength bands with greater precision than older Landsat satellites. It can sense slight differences in color in dense forests or water. Landsat 9 also has a Thermal Infrared Sensor (TIRS) to detect subtle differences in heat radiating from Earth. Landsat 9 combines OLI and TIRS data to produce highly detailed snapshots of Earth. False colors added by computers accentuate features to highlight them.

WEATHER FORECASTING

Forecasting weather is a predictive science using atmospheric data. Some data come from weather stations on the ground or in Earth's atmosphere. But today, about 90 percent of weather data comes from sensors on satellites. The global fleet of modern weather satellites is constantly updated. Today, advanced weather satellites are necessary to meet the increasing demand for nowcasting—short-range, highly precise weather forecasting for specific locations.

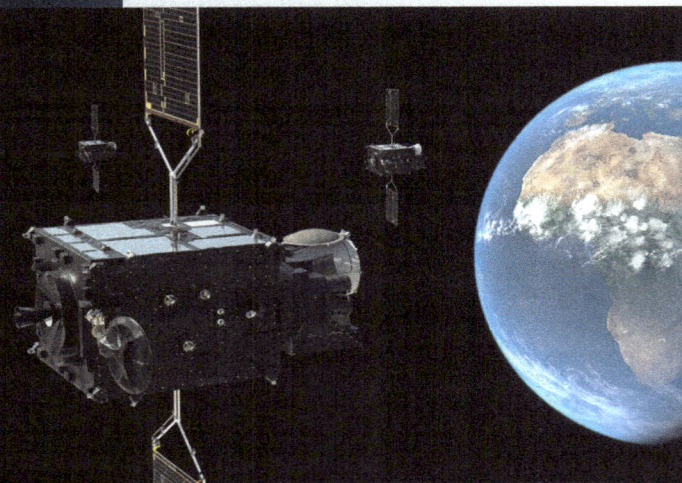

Storm alert. Lightning often precedes a dangerous thunderstorm or other extreme weather. The newest MTG-I1 weather satellites are equipped with sensors that can detect a single lightning flash. They can differentiate cloud-to-cloud, cloud-to-ground, and lightning within a cloud features beyond the capability of ground-based lightning stations. The sensors on MTG-I1 detect the optical (visible) pulses from lightning. Predictive software combines this data with rainfall and cloud data into nowcasts that provide early warnings of storms and other severe weather.

Deep generative models (DGM's) are numerical weather prediction tools that can deliver more accurate nowcasting. A DGM uses **machine learning** to make detailed rainfall predictions by comparing radar data to past radar data instead of traditional meteorological calculations. Radar data is collected every 5 minutes from satellites at a resolution of around 3 miles (5 kilometers). Using these data, DGM can more accurately capture the circulation, intensity, and structure of storms—important features used to generate a precise nowcast.

Hurricane watch. In 2023, scientists plan to use a swarm of four CubeSats deployed into LEO to measure the 3D structure and strength of cyclones and hurricanes. The Time-Resolved Observations of Precipitation Structure and Storm Intensity with a Constellation of Smallsats (TROPICS) mission will remotely sense the vertical and horizontal distribution of temperature and humidity readings within the storms and the surrounding environment. Data from TROPICS is updated constantly. This will help accurately calculate where a storm will make landfall and estimate potential storm damage.

The weather of things. The private weather forecasting industry is made up of companies that repackage weather data obtained from national weather agencies. The data is often several days old. Tomorrow.io is a new weather forecasting company that uses technology to combine data from satellites, weather stations, ocean buoys, and cell phone towers with data from various devices connected via the internet. For example, advanced windshield wipers on new cars may transmit data wirelessly in response to rain. The widespread network of everyday items connected through wireless internet is called The Internet of Things. Tomorrow.io plans to launch 30 weather satellites to record data over oceans and detect activity that land-directed weather satellites often neglect. Combining that data with weather information detected in everyday devices creates a new "weather of things." The mass of data allows Tomorrow.io to tailor forecasts to sell to specific industries that require accurate weather prediction, such as transportation and sports.

MONITORING CLIMATE CHANGE

Today, essential climate variables (ECV) data are mostly measured from space by advanced satellites. For scientists, ECVs are key to assessing climate change and its impacts. Scientists monitor ECV data to study desertification, air pollution, and changes in ice cover in Earth's polar regions. Scientists are closely monitoring regions where melting polar ice is driving sea-level rise and where permafrost is melting. These are caused by global warming. Today, the Reference Elevation Model of Antarctica (REMA) maps changes in the Antarctic ice in finer detail than ever before.

Antarctic relief. REMA combines high-resolution images of Antarctica's ice with Digital Elevation Model (DEM) data, recorded mainly from WorldView satellites between 2009 and 2021. The model compares the data to measure changes in relief (surface differences). The incredible amount of data (around 150 terabytes) was stitched together using a powerful supercomputer to produce a scalable (changeable) map. New data continually update the map to detect changes in relief. Such changes may be caused by ice melt and stress fractures in the Antarctic ice shelf that lead to the breakup of glaciers.

Hyperspectral imager. The newest satellite sensors can image a wider range of the light spectrum to deliver more accurate ECV data. The Copernicus Hyperspectral Imaging Mission for the Environment (CHIME) satellites have hyperspectral imagers that separate incoming light into different wavelengths. Conventional systems assign a single primary color value to each pixel (picture element) in an image. The new hyperspectral imager collects detailed spectral (light) information for every pixel. This provides amazingly detailed images that help scientists recognize the impacts of climate change and environmental degradation. The European Space Agency (ESA) plans to add CHIME satellites to its Sentinel program of Earth-observing satellites for future missions.

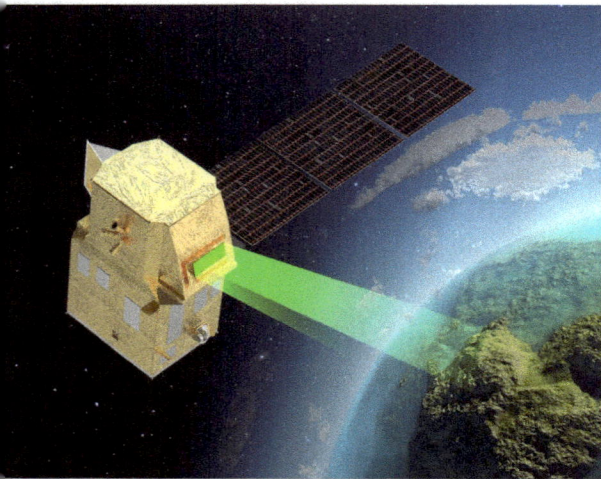

Greenhouse gas watch. France's National Center for Space Studies (CNES) will launch its MicroCarb satellite mission in 2024 to monitor atmospheric carbon dioxide (CO_2), the main **greenhouse gas.** The MicroCarb sensors measure atmospheric changes in CO_2 on a global scale. It can zoom in to monitor a specific location using a "CityMode" to measure CO_2 levels with 1 square mile (2.5 square kilometers) resolution. MicroCarb data will be used to advise national and local governments on CO_2 emissions to inform decisions on reducing emissions. The private Kayrros geoanalytics company uses ECV data to map methane bombs—sites where the emission of methane, a powerful greenhouse gas, is especially high. Many methane bombs are sites where energy companies are extracting oil or natural gas.

Geoengineering. Scientists are developing ways to use advanced satellites in geoengineering—large-scale human interventions in Earth's natural systems to counter climate change and extreme weather. One idea is to beam microwaves from satellites to warm the clouds in developing hurricanes. Some experts think that this may stop a hurricane in its tracks. Another concept is to blast moon dust into Earth's orbit from lunar satellite platforms to create a solar shield for Earth and reduce global temperatures! Geostorm, a science fiction film, imagined the catastrophic results that occur when a futuristic constellation of weather control satellites malfunction.

GROUND VIEWS

High-tech satellite remote sensors can map the ground in astonishing detail. Their images may show surface changes that occur with urban development and temperature distribution, such as heat islands, in cities. They can detect dangerous algal blooms in lakes and assess forest health. For example, Global Forest Watch (GFW) is a free interactive online forest monitoring and alert system that uses high-resolution radar imaging from satellites to spot deforestation.

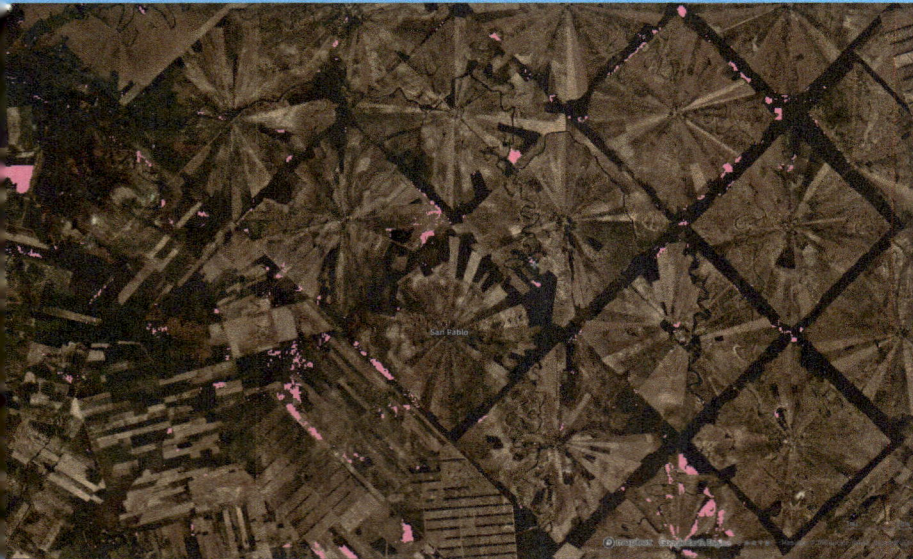

Through the clouds. Global Forest Watch uses Radar for Detecting Deforestation (RADD). These sensors on modern French Sentinel-1 satellites can detect changes within 30 feet (10 meters). This is nine times more detailed than optical sensors on older Landsat satellites. RADD can image a single tree in a forest. RADD signals penetrate the cloud cover that usually occurs over tropical forests. RADD data is updated every 6 to 12 days. Older satellites and optical systems may take weeks to wait for cloud-free days to monitor forests. GFW issues an alert whenever a decline in forest cover is registered at any scale. Forest monitors use the alerts to address deforestation in environmentally sensitive and protected areas.

Crop sensing by satellite monitoring saves time and resources for farmers. Today's advanced satellites have sensors that can estimate crop yields by monitoring color, leaf cover, or plant height. Computers compare the data with historical seasonal variation. Farmers use the information to decide when to irrigate fields, apply fertilizer or pesticides, or harvest crops. This method is less time-consuming than inspecting crops manually.

Water audit. NASA's 2022 Surface Water and Ocean Topography (SWOT) satellite surveys nearly all of Earth's lakes, rivers, reservoirs, and oceans every 21 days. This is the first global audit of water resources conducted from space. SWOT's payload includes a Ka-band radio interferometer (a device that uses light waves to make precise measurements) to measure sea levels and a microwave radiometer to detect water vapor in the atmosphere. SWOT data is used to monitor ocean circulation that affects weather, monitor rising ocean levels, and inform officials on freshwater management.

Satellite prospecting uses satellites to observe the geology of an area and discover valuable minerals. The Australian company Fleet Space developed its ExoSphere satellite prospecting system using a network of ground sensors called Geodes. Geodes are embedded in the land surface. They use ambient noise tomography, where sound waves reveal subsurface structures. Geodes can discover deposits of useful minerals, such as lithium, which is used in advanced batteries. The Geodes uplink data to LEO satellites. The data is used to make accurate mineralogical maps for mining companies. Satellite prospecting avoids the unnecessary environmental damage from traditional prospecting and mining.

5 OBSERVING SPACE

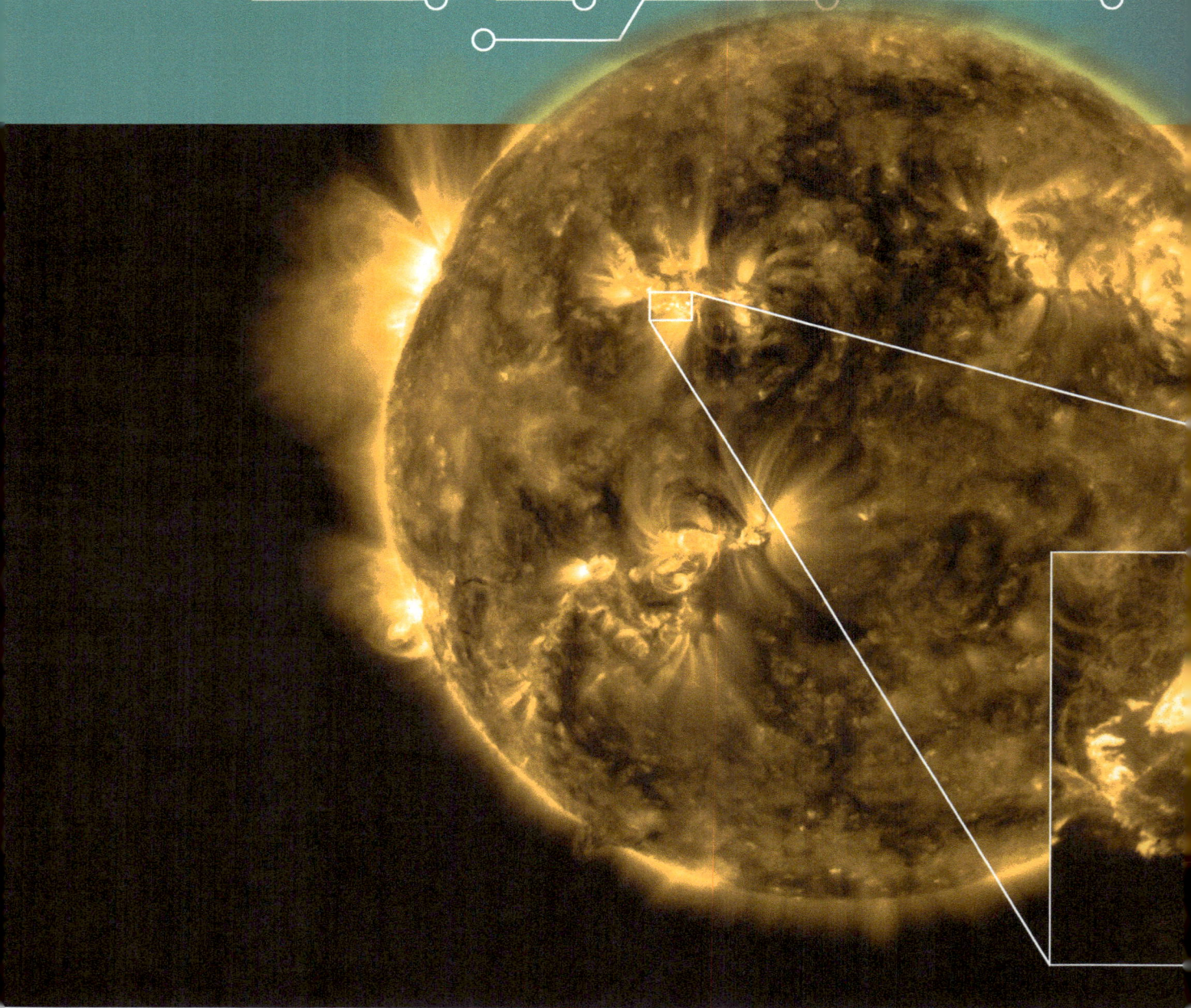

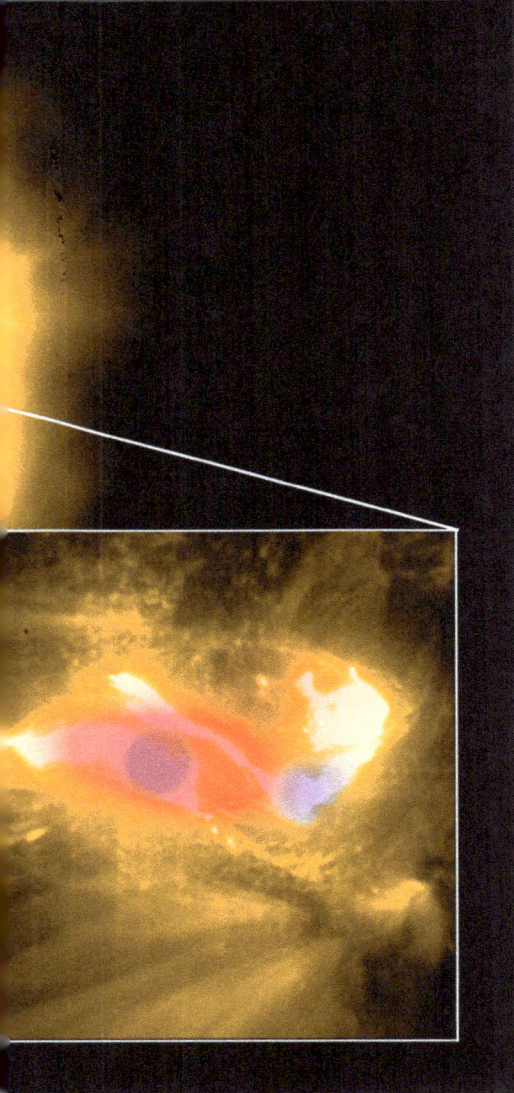

STARGAZING

Modern satellite observatories provide astronomers with a clearer view of the universe compared to Earth-based telescopes. In space, there is no light pollution, cloud cover, or distortion from Earth's atmosphere. Space telescopes are revolutionizing astronomy and helping scientists understand how the universe works and perhaps discover signs of alien life. Other satellites point their specialized sensors toward the sun, our nearest star.

The ESA's Solar Orbiter mission is the most advanced space laboratory to study the sun. Launched in 2020, it observes the behavior of the sun. Solar Orbiter circles the sun every six months, coming within 26 million miles (42 million kilometers) of the surface. Solar Orbiter has a carbon fiber composite heat shield to withstand the incredible heat from the sun, which is about 13 times that experienced by Earth-orbiting satellites. The heat shield allows some sunlight to reach the sensors. But precise controls avoid damaging the sensitive instruments. Sensors include an extreme ultraviolet imager to capture detailed images of solar flares—huge pulses of plasma blasting from the sun's surface.

SPACE TELESCOPES

For decades, the Hubble Space Telescope was the highest-performing space telescope, providing the first images of the birth and death of stars! It imaged mostly visible and ultraviolet (UV) light. But Hubble's sensors could not detect more distant objects with great clarity. Light from such objects is pushed from the visible and UV wavelengths to the near infrared by clouds of dust. Scientists at NASA, ESA, and the Canadian Space Agency (CSA) built the James Webb Space Telescope (JWST) as an infrared specialist. JWST was launched into space atop an Ariane 5 rocket in late 2021. It began observations in 2022.

Miraculous mirror. JWST's remarkable light-gathering ability relies on its enormous primary mirror , which measures more than 21 feet (6.5 meters) across. The mirror reflects and concentrates visible light onto a secondary mirror that bounces it to JWST's sensor payload. It was a real challenge to launch such a big mirror into space. Scientists solved this problem by constructing the JWST mirror from 18 hexagonal panels of strong, lightweight beryllium coated in gold. The panels were folded for launch and opened once the JWST reached orbit. Actuators behind the panels can move and bend the mirror by amounts much smaller than the width of a human hair to focus light precisely.

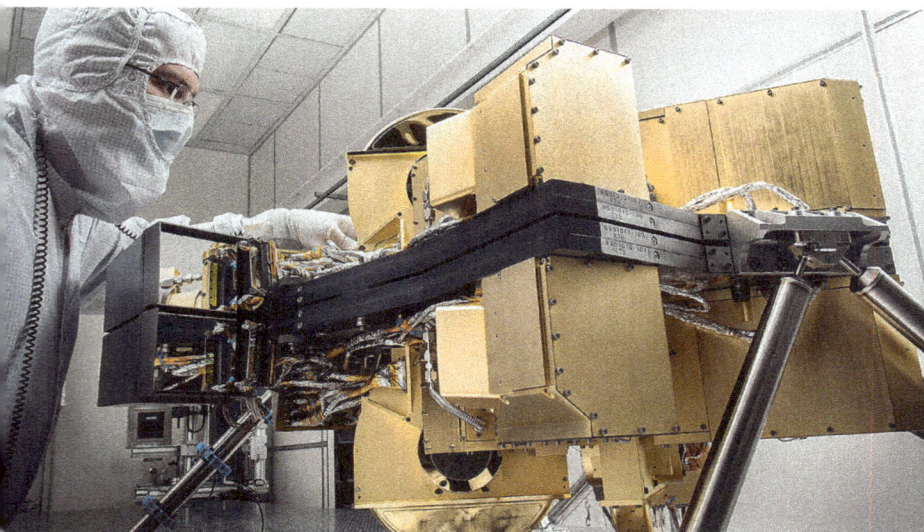

NIRCam (Near Infrared Camera) is the JWST's primary imager. It holds 10 sensor arrays that act like the charge-coupled devices that turn light into digital data in a digital camera. The arrays detect infrared wavelengths ranging from 0.6 to 5 microns. A coronagraph blocks the light of a brighter object, so dim objects nearby can be viewed. The coronagraph allows astronomers to discover dim planets orbiting distant stars.

Keeping cool. Instruments on the JWST must be kept cool to –370 °F (50 Kelvin) to detect faint infrared emissions from distant objects. A large sun shield the size of a tennis court faces the sun to shade the JWST mirror and sensors from the heat. The shield uses layers of shiny kapton, the material used for space blankets, to reflect heat. Other sensors that detect longer wavelengths and mid-infrared light must be kept even colder to prevent electronic signal noise. A cryocooler maintains the sensors at –448 °F (about 5 K)! A bit like a household freezer, a cooling system on the JWST pumps cold helium gas to a heat exchanger in the cryocooler.

Dark energy. One of the greatest mysteries in astronomy is why the universe is expanding at an increasingly fast rate. Astronomers think dark energy could be the cause. But the effects of this weak, invisible pressure can only be observed at an intergalactic scale. New high-tech telescopes are planned to solve the mystery of dark energy. NASA's Nancy Grace Roman Space Telescope, due for launch in 2027, will have a wide-field camera with over 300-megapixel resolution to observe at an intergalactic scale. This advanced telescope will help astronomers image features of dark energy in action.

SPACE SATELLITES AT WORK

Space exploration will depend on advances in satellite technology. Space scientists plan to use the moon as a staging point for future human missions into deep space. Other advanced satellites are collecting valuable data from Mars, searching for planets beyond our solar system, and even helping protect Earth.

Blazing a trail. NASA's CAPSTONE and Flashlight satellite missions were launched in 2022 to begin this new era in space exploration. CAPSTONE is a 12U CubeSat launched to orbit the moon. The CubeSat will test new navigation systems and help calculate the best orbital path for the future Gateway space station that will orbit the Moon. NASA plans to use Gateway and a human base on the moon to launch spacecraft into deep space beyond the moon and to Mars.

Shedding new light. The Lunar Flashlight satellite is a briefcase-sized 6U CubeSat launched in 2022 to map regions at the lunar south pole. Here, parts of the lunar surface are permanently in shadow and covered with water ice. Lunar Flashlight has a laser reflectometer that shines laser light onto the lunar surface and records the reflection. Scientists need to know how much ice exists on the moon. They plan to use the ice for drinking water and to generate oxygen and fuel for a moon base.

Landing on Mars. NASA's twin ESCAPADE satellites will launch on a 2024 rideshare rocket to study the Martian atmosphere in preparation for a human mission. Data from the ESCAPADE satellites could be key to a safe landing on and departure from Mars in the future.

Planetary defense. In 2022, NASA's DART spacecraft crashed into a speeding asteroid. The impact altered the asteroid's orbit by a small amount. This mission to demonstrate the use of spacecraft in planetary defense was accompanied by the Italian Space Agency's (ISA) 6U CubeSat, LICIACube. LICIACube sent images of the impact to scientists on Earth. Results recorded by LICIACube will inform Earth's response to any asteroid threat in the future.

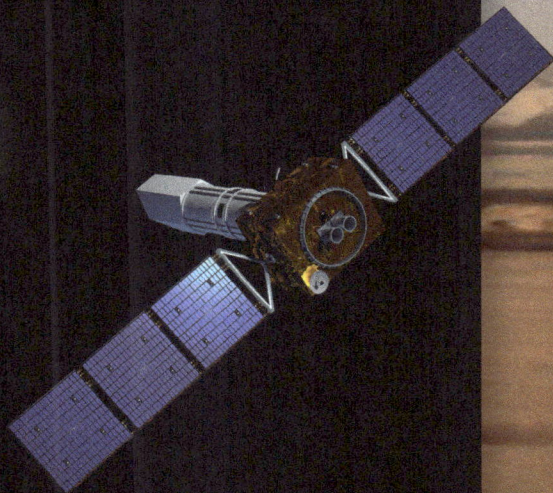

Exoplanets are planets that orbit distant stars. THE JWST has already produced blurry images of faraway exoplanets. NASA's planned Habitable Exoplanet Observatory (HabEx) will directly image exoplanets and search for signs of life in the universe. Planned for a 2035 launch, HabEx will use spectroscopes to detect water and atmospheric gases, such as oxygen, that suggest biological activity. The two-piece concept for HabEx is a sensitive space telescope with an enormous star shield orbiting thousands of miles beyond Earth! The star shield will block light from a star, so that the telescope can image and survey its exoplanets.

ENGAGE YOUR READER

Nonfiction writing often includes subject-specific vocabulary terms. Knowing the words related to the topic helps us understand the text itself.

When good readers come upon words they don't know well, they pause and try to figure them out. One tool they use is the glossary, like the one on page 4. Not every word can be defined in a glossary, though!

Authors know this, so they leave clues about words in the text. Next time you encounter a challenging word, stop and look for information about its meaning in the surrounding sentences. Sometimes authors define the term right there in the text! Other times, they'll compare the term to something you may already know. Authors even use punctuation like commas or dashes to clue you in to a word's meaning.

INSTRUCTIONS

1. Consider the list of challenge words and identify where each is used in the text. You can use the Index on page 48 to help you locate each term.

2. Explain how the author described each word. Ask yourself "what is happening in the text?" or "how is this word being used?" as you search for clues about their meanings.

3. Create your own definitions of the words. Don't just copy the dictionary definitions. Instead think about how you would tell a friend what each term means.

4. Add a visual representation for each word. Think about what you could draw that will help you remember what the words mean.

CHALLENGE WORDS

- CubeSat
- Payload
- Low Earth Orbit (LEO)
- Bus

- Telecommunication
- Latency
- Satellite constellation
- Global Navigation Satellite Systems (GNSS)

EXAMPLE

Challenge Word	Page(s)	Author's Description	Personal Definition	Visual Representation
CubeSat	5, 7	- cube-shaped class of tiny satellites called nanosatellites - built from commercial rather than custom parts - launched into orbit to complete a wide variety of tasks	A cube-shaped nanosatellite weighing just a few pounds. Purposely small to offset the costs of getting it into orbit to perform a variety of tasks.	
Payload				

INDEX

A
aircraft, 18, 24
antennae, 17, 18, 19, 26, 29,
atmospheres, 8, 13, 20, 29, 34, 37, 39, 41, 44
autonomous(ly), 12, 20,

B
BeiDou, 22, 23, 28

C
Chinese Space Station (CSS), 14, 15
climate change, 33, 36, 37
communications, 13, 18, 19, 20, 29
composite, 10, 41
constellation, 20, 21, 22, 23, 35, 37
CubeSats, 7-9, 10-13, 15, 19, 21, 35, 44, 45

D
debris, 10, 29
downlink, 18, 25, 30
drones, 25, 26

E
earthquakes, 30, 31
encryption, 20, 27

F
fiber optic, 11, 27
forecasts, 34, 35
frequencies, 18, 19

G
Global Navigation Satellite Systems (GNSS), 23-26, 28-30
Global Positioning System (GPS), 23, 25-31
gravity, 7, 15
ground stations, 18, 23

H
hurricanes, 35, 37

I
infrared, 12, 18, 33, 42, 43

International Space Station (ISS), 9, 15, 29

J
James Webb Space Telescope (JWST), 42, 43
jamming, 26, 27, 29

L
Landsat (satellite), 33, 38
lasers, 18, 24, 27, 44
latency, 18, 20
launch vehicles, 8, 9, 20
Low Earth Orbit (LEO), 8, 10, 14, 15, 18, 20, 35, 39

M
Mars, 8, 13, 44
microwaves, 24, 37
modular, 7, 9, 15
modules, 12, 14, 15
moon, 8, 15, 44

N
National Aeronautics and Space Administration (NASA), 12, 13, 15, 18, 39, 42-45
navigation, 22-24, 27, 28
networks, 15, 20, 23, 25, 27, 31, 35, 39

O
optical, 18, 24, 34, 38
orbits, 7-9, 13, 14, 15, 20, 28, 29, 37, 42, 45

P
payloads, 7, 8, 9, 10, 12, 19, 28, 33, 39, 42
position, navigation and timing (PNT), 24-26, 30

R
radar, 34, 38
radiation, 10, 12, 33
radio waves, 17-19

receivers, 17, 24, 26
remote sensing, 33, 38
rideshare, 9, 30, 44
robotic arms, 9, 15
rockets, 8, 14, 20, 29, 42, 44

S
satellites, 7-9, 12-14, 17-30, 33-39, 41, 44
sensors, 10-12, 20, 25, 29, 34, 36-39, 41-43
signals, 17-19, 23, 24, 26, 27, 29, 38
smart, 11, 25, 30
smartphones, 7, 19, 31
software, 10, 11, 25, 26, 28, 34
solar arrays, 10, 19, 28
solar cells, 10, 11
space junk, 13, 20
space telescopes, 42, 43, 45
spacecraft, 10, 13, 15, 18, 44, 45
SpaceX, 8, 20, 21
spoofing, 26, 27, 29
streaming, 7, 17, 21, 27
sun, 10, 11, 41, 43
swarms, 12, 21, 35
synchronization, 24, 25, 27

T
telecommunication (telecom), 16-19, 20, 21
3D printing, 10, 29
tracking, 30, 31
transmission, 18, 23

U
ultraviolet, 41, 42
Universal Coordinated Time (UTC), 24, 27
universe, 41, 43, 45

W
wavelengths, 17, 18, 33, 36, 42, 43
wireless, 14, 18, 25, 27, 30, 35

www.ingramcontent.com/pod-product-compliance
Lightning Source LLC
Chambersburg PA
CBHW061420090426
42744CB00018B/2076